TAKE, BLESS, BREAK, SHARE

CARDINAL BLASE J. CUPICH

TAKE, Bless, BREAK, Share

A STRATEGY *for* *a* EUCHARISTIC REVIVAL

TWENTY-THIRD PUBLICATIONS

twentythirdpublications.com

TWENTY-THIRD PUBLICATIONS
One Montauk Avenue
New London, CT 06320
(860) 437-3012 or (800) 321-0411
www.twentythirdpublications.com

A shorter version of this text first appeared on
September 12, 2021 in *Commonweal* Magazine.

Image credit: ©stock.adobe.com

ISBN: 978-1-62785-694-2
Printed in the U.S.A.

bayard A Division of Bayard, Inc.

Contents

How to Use This Resource

These reflections can be used for individual reflection and prayer but are also fruitful when used in a group setting in order to promote conversation and sharing. For those who wish, here is a simple process for group use:

GATHER and welcome everyone, invite introductions. Begin with the sign of the cross, asking God to bless your time together and send the Spirit to guide you.

READ the material in each section, rotating readers, if desired. Pause for quiet reflection before entering into conversation.

DISCUSS the material, using any of the suggested questions as a starting point and adding others that may arise.

FINISH the time together by inviting participants to consider what ideas resonated most and what new insights were gained. Ask them to identify one or two large ideas that they will take away from the time together that might inspire new practices in their homes or parishes.

CONCLUDE with a brief prayer and hospitality, reminding everyone that "where two or three are gathered" (Matthew 18:20), Jesus has promised to be present.

Welcome

AN INVITATION TO WORSHIP

In the gift of the Eucharist, Jesus left his disciples with a way to enter into the mystery of his life, death, and resurrection. In every eucharistic liturgy, we gather with others as the Body of Christ *in community* to celebrate the Body of Christ. Noisy and harsh divisions, conflicting headlines vying for attention, viewpoints demanding our loyalty: these can distract, distress, and dull our appreciation of the unity and solidarity offered in the Eucharist. Perhaps it is time to renew our appreciation for this great gift, and to revive the connection between the Eucharist and the ways we "live and move and have our being" (Acts 17:28) in today's complex world.

1

The essential starting point for developing a strategy designed to support a Eucharistic revival in our Church must be the needs of Catholics today. Context is key. Those involved in catechesis and faith formation should make every effort to avoid an ahistorical presentation of the Eucharist that is disconnected from daily life. With that in mind, I offer five themes that might be considered in shaping a process that invites dialogue among the faithful and reflects the personal, pastoral, catechetical, and formational challenges that are specific to our U.S. context today: the imperative to worship; the necessity of the Eucharist; the Eucharist as call to participation; the Eucharist as model of self-giving; the Eucharist as the sacrament of the Lord's abiding presence.

ONE

The Imperative of Worship

IN CATHOLIC TRADITION, THE EUCHARIST IS THE CEN-
TRAL ACT OF WORSHIP THAT SUSTAINS THE LIFE OF
FAITH. Worship itself, however, is often marginalized in
a culture that is driven by deep-seated commitments to
individual freedom, self-fulfillment, and self-expression.

In practice, Americans, including many Catholics, view
worship as one choice among many, something one does
if one so desires, or has time. My predecessor in Chicago,
Cardinal Francis George, OMI, suggested that many
people, again including Catholics, put Sunday worship on
par with other recreational choices or tasks to complete. If
one has the time and inclination, one will go to church—

or, if not, choose to go shopping, do laundry, or watch football. And while our daily tasks are certainly important and may even be fulfilling, how do we help people grasp that the Eucharist is truly the "source and summit" of our lives in Christ? Further, how might we create an atmosphere in which encountering the risen Christ in the Eucharist is an essential part of our week?

If Eucharistic formation, catechesis, and revival are to happen, then all members of the Church community, as well as its leaders, must address this fundamental question of worship: Is it, in fact, optional or is it necessary? And how might those of us who are church leaders help ensure that the vital importance of the liturgy is reflected in our words and actions?

In Catholic catechesis, the Sunday obligation has traditionally had its roots in the Third Commandment, "Remember to keep holy the Lord's Day." Of course, keeping holy the Lord's Day entails worship. But perhaps the obligation and, even more, the necessity of Sunday worship is more tied to the First Commandment: "You shall not have false gods before me." Inevitably, we will worship because there is something in our nature that moves us to awe and surrender before something greater than ourselves. The question, however, is what or whom will we worship? In a self-referential age plagued by all kinds of addictions and a (not unrelated) thick culture of consumerism, our worship can sometimes steer us away from God. The ever-present danger in this moment is idolatry. Consequently, if we are to spare ourselves the entrapments of the many idols that mark our lives, then worship of God is necessary. Indeed, there is a Eucharistic imperative: The Eucharist is essential to our lives as Catholics. And this is a second and related theme of the vital importance of the Eucharist.

For Reflection *and* Conversation

1. When I participate in Eucharistic worship, how is my spirit enriched and enlivened? When I experience the liturgy, do I fully grasp that I am worshiping with a community of believers, both living and dead, in the presence of God?

2. Consider the difference between the "obligation" to worship on Sundays and the "necessity." What does this distinction suggest? How does our communal experience of the liturgy reflect this sense of its *necessity* to our Catholic living?

3. Which "self-referential" aspects of contemporary culture might leave me isolated and disconnected from my community of neighbors and colleagues? What aspects of contemporary culture actually support my faith and spirituality and connect me to community?

4. How does participation in worship help me to refocus my attention on what truly matters in my life as well as in the lives of others?

The Eucharist as a Matter of Life and Death

AMERICANS MIGHT BE ABLE TO COMPREHEND THE GREAT IMPORTANCE OF WORSHIP, but to characterize the Eucharist as a matter of life and death may seem to be an excessively dramatic description. In fact, the words of Jesus support this vital sense of the Eucharist and Eucharistic worship: "Jesus said to them, 'Amen, amen, I say to you, unless you eat the flesh of the Son of Man and drink his blood, you do not have life within you.

Whoever eats my flesh and drinks my blood has eternal life, and I will raise him on the last day'" (John 6:53–54).

We need to take Jesus at his word. Any Eucharistic revival, supported by formation and catechesis, must have a strong biblical base in the words and actions of Jesus. This passage from John 6 illustrates the importance of staying close to the Word as a means of staying close to the Eucharist. And the words of Jesus about the bread of life clearly resonate in these trying days when death-dealing forces appear to have the upper hand. Think of the pandemic, the street violence and killing that plague our cities, the disrespect for human life in its most vulnerable stages and conditions, the lethal degradation of the environment, and the specter of war that haunts the world. An essential task for people of faith and for those of us who share our faith with others is to draw a line from the deadly challenges we face today to the Eucharist as the bread of *life*.

For Reflection *and* Conversation

1. Jesus says that anyone who does not partake of his body and blood will not have life within. How does participation in the liturgy affect my own "inner life"?

2. Think about the nourishment received from food and how it supports the body's flourishing. How does the Eucharist nourish my spiritual life so that I experience inner flourishing?

3. What is one "death-dealing challenge" I face in my own life, family, or community? How might the bread of *life* help me to overcome this challenge and offer another way of living?

4. How might our worshiping community become a transformative force of resurrection and new life in the world?

THREE

The Eucharist as Summons to Participation

THE HEART OF THE EUCHARISTIC PRAYERS WE HEAR AT MASS INCLUDES FOUR ACTIONS THAT WE ARE TO PERFORM IN MEMORY OF JESUS: *he took bread, blessed it, broke it, and gave it.* The Eucharist is not fundamentally a static reality. In a primary sense, the Eucharist is action or an event, the Lord's action in his Paschal Mystery, that summons our participation.

At the beginning of the twentieth century, Pope St. Pius X identified the essential nature of liturgical participation. He said that the first and foremost source of the Christian life is active participation in the liturgy. This summons to active participation developed across the twentieth century and culminated in the directions offered in the Second Vatican Council's *Constitution on the Sacred Liturgy*. The Council identified the internal and external aspects of participation and its dimensions as active, conscious, full, and fruitful.

Some sixty years after the promulgation of this document on the liturgy, many Catholics may not know their call to active participation in the eucharistic mysteries and they may not have made an intentional commitment to it. For some, active participation seems to mean having a particular role to play in the liturgy (greeter, server, lector, Communion minister). Yet, all Catholics are called to full and conscious participation that means internally joining ourselves to the death and resurrection of the Lord celebrated in the Eucharist.

In place of active participation, some seem to view their engagement with Eucharistic worship in a number of other ways: the mere fulfillment of an obligation, a private, meditative moment in their otherwise busy lives, or as an opportunity to receive personal inspiration or encouragement. How many of our Catholic brothers and sisters seem to conceive of the liturgy as a spectator sport? How often do we hear, "But I don't get anything out of it"?

Any effective Eucharistic revival must include catechesis and formation, and must take into account not only the Eucharist in itself but also our response to the Eucharist. That means helping people understand what active participation in the Eucharist means, and working within our faith communities to develop a liturgical experience that is both local and universal and that fits the culture and climate of our parishes.

For Reflection *and* Conversation

1. In giving us the Eucharist, Jesus "took, blessed, broke, and gave." How do these actions resonate with me? In what way can I put this into practice in my life and in my relationships?

2. How do I understand "full participation" in the Eucharistic liturgy? In what ways might I engage in the liturgy more vibrantly? How could my community better encourage full participation?

3. "But I don't get anything out of Mass." Do I or someone I know feel this way at times? If so, what might shift that perspective? How can we, as a faith community, better listen to and address the reasons people may feel less than fulfilled at Mass?

4. In the end, the liturgy is about encountering the person of Jesus Christ. Which aspects of the liturgy most support this encounter for me? How could I enhance that personal encounter? How can I offer this encounter to others?

From the Sacrifice of Jesus to Our Sacrificial Living

ACTIVE PARTICIPATION MUST ALSO BE *FRUITFUL* PARTIC-IPATION. As we join ourselves to the self-sacrificing love of Jesus manifested on the Cross, we are called to replicate his sacrifice in our daily lives. When we do that, we live out his mission through our decisions, actions, and relationships. The sacrifice of Jesus encountered in the

Eucharist is both the model for our lives and also what enables our self-sacrificing love.

How might we help Catholics truly grasp that the Eucharist necessarily leads us out of the liturgy into ordinary life, where we enact what we have celebrated? Our context may be marriage and family, the workplace, the wider community, and even the natural world itself. More commonly, people tend to view the Eucharistic celebration as self-contained, whose lessons and imperatives can be safely left in church until next Sunday. Yet true participation in the Eucharist necessarily shapes our moral choices, orienting us to serve those in need and guiding us to strengthen relationships.

Americans can tend to live largely compartmentalized lives. We often feel comfortable separating realms of living—for example, the private, public, religious, civic, financial, or recreational. The Eucharist, however, calls us to an *integrated* life marked by the same self-sacrificing love that is celebrated as the great mystery of our faith. In effect, the challenge of a Eucharistic revival in this context is really a challenge of imagination. We are invited to re-imagine our lives as oriented toward unity and integration through the Eucharist. It is for this reason that great care should be given not to make the Body and Blood of Christ into an object we control. No, active participation in Eucharistic worship is, rather, the primary way in which we experience our transformation in Christ.

For Reflection *and* Conversation

1. Consider the connection between the self-sacrificing love of Jesus on the Cross and the Eucharist. How might my encounter with the risen Jesus in the Eucharist enable my own self-sacrificing love?

2. What events in my daily life are most directly supported by my Eucharistic participation? Are there ways I feel called to better connect daily life and weekly worship?

3. How can participation in the Eucharist influence my most important relationships? My circle of friends? My wider community? What areas need growth? What might a more intentional connection between daily life and Eucharistic participation look like?

4. "The Eucharist invites us to re-imagine life through the lens of unity." What would "more unity" in my life look like? In our parish? In our diocese? In what ways might we be a force for unity in our community and world?

FIVE

The Eucharist Is the Sacrament of the Lord's Abiding Presence

EUCHARISTIC ADORATION IS A LEGITIMATE DEVELOP-
MENT OF PIETY IN THE WESTERN CHURCH WITH MANY
BENEFITS FOR THOSE WHO ENGAGE IN IT. Adoration high-
lights the abiding presence of the Lord in his sacrament.
And with that sense of presence, we also grasp his avail-
ability to us. As a spiritual practice, adoration offers an

opportunity for quiet and meditative prayer focused on the Lord present in his sacrament. In recent decades, this form of prayer has gained followers in the United States for whom it has become a very important dimension of their spirituality.

And although there are many positive elements in Eucharistic adoration, it also needs the context and direction of Eucharistic catechesis and formation to avoid narrowness and even distorted perceptions of the sacrament itself. For example, without the proper context, Eucharistic adoration can privatize one's relationship to the sacrament and to the Lord himself, overlooking the communitarian dimension of Eucharistic worship, and our responsibility to engage with our community in an active way. Although the prayer associated with adoration can and should be personal, it cannot be merely private and authentically Eucharistic at the same time. The liturgical books that offer the pathway for adoration assume a community context—proclamation of the Word of God, perhaps some music, and a common gathering of the faithful for adoration. Similarly, adoration cannot "objectify" the Eucharist, making it a static reality. Adoration must come from and lead to the Eucharistic celebration. It is never detached or entirely separated from the liturgical celebration.

These concerns about Eucharistic adoration also apply to various forms of popular piety that have a Eucharistic dimension. Those responsible for catechesis and formation within the community and families must highlight the link between the Eucharistic liturgy and devotional practices. That same catechesis and formation should also encourage these manifestations of popular piety and prayer practices to maintain and even strengthen their communal or community character.

For Reflection *and* Conversation

1. Besides participation in the liturgy, are there other forms of Eucharistic piety that speak to me? What makes them special or appealing?

2. Have I participated in Eucharistic adoration? What was my experience of "Jesus making himself available" through that encounter? How did that experience connect me to the wider community of believers?

3. How might we take steps to avoid separating Eucharistic devotions from the celebration of the liturgy? Is this an area where growth in our parish might be needed?

4. What connections can I make between experiencing Jesus as the bread of life, and my own call to be "bread for the life of the world"? That is, in what ways can I live a Eucharistic life that promotes truth, justice, compassion, charity, service and radical reverence in my everyday life and in my community's experience?

Sending Forth:

EUCHARIST FOR THE LIFE

OF THE WORLD

Catholics, including bishops, leaders at all levels, and all the faithful, should give the Eucharistic Mystery the time and attention it deserves, as our singular aim must be serving our community—the people of God—in a way that builds up the Body of Christ. Without doubt, a Eucharistic revival needs to address the particular cultural-historical context and the relevant questions that belong to this moment in American life. But if a strategy for revival is to be successful, it must be grounded in a robust and sound theology that reminds us what the Eucharist means, not only for our practice of worship, but also for how we leaven the world the Lord made us for.

Jesus told his followers, "This is how all will know that you are my disciples: if you have love for one another" (John 13:35). May our love for one another be strengthened and nourished by our celebration of the Eucharistic mystery together, and may this love be a source of unity and healing for the life of the world.